CCSS Genre Fiction

 Essential Question
What excites us about nature?

Star Party

by Betsy Hebert

illustrated by Margeaux Lucas

CHAPTER 1

Getting Ready

Cassie opened the back door and stepped onto the patio. She looked up at the sky, which was growing darker, but it still wasn't dark enough.

"Sweetie," her father said, "I told you it wouldn't be dark enough for another half an hour. Opening and closing the door every five minutes is not going to make it get dark faster. All it's going to do is make the house get colder."

"I know," Cassie said, "but I'm really looking forward to the star party."

Cassie reluctantly went inside. "When will everybody get here?" she asked.

"They'll be here soon, honey," Mom responded. "In the meantime, please go and get your brother."

Cassie went upstairs to look for her brother, Marcos. She was pretty sure she knew where he would be. When she opened the door to his room, she saw that she was right.

Marcos, who was six, was under the covers of his top bunk. He had a book and a flashlight that Cassie could see shining through the bedspread.

"Hey, Marcos, it's almost time for the star party," Cassie said. "It's a great night for it, too. The moon is new and not too bright, so we should be able to see a lot. We might even see meteors flash across the night sky—you know, shooting stars!"

Her brother, however, did not share Cassie's excitement. "I'm not going to the party," he said, his voice muffled by the covers. "You know I don't like the dark."

Of course, Cassie knew how Marcos felt, but she'd been trying to change his mind. She knew if he'd only give it a chance, the idea of a star party would excite him, too.

"It's not scary at all," Cassie said gently.

Marcos poked his head out and glared at his sister. "I *know* that," he said angrily. "I'm not scared. I just don't like the dark." Then he pulled the covers up over his head again and repeated, "I'm not going to the party."

Dad had joined Cassie in the doorway in time to hear Marcos's last comment. He walked to the bunk and pulled back the covers.

✳ ✳ ✳ CHAPTER 2 ✳ ✳ ✳
A Deal

"Why don't we make a deal?" Dad said to Marcos. "You come to the party for ten minutes to listen to Cassie, say hi to our guests, and look through the telescope. If you still want to come inside after that, you can."

Marcos looked at Dad. "Only ten minutes?" he asked.

Dad nodded, and so did Cassie.

Marcos took a deep breath and started to climb down. "Can I bring my flashlight outdoors?" he asked.

"No, buddy, I'm sorry," Dad said. "We can't have any lights on out there because that makes it hard to see the sky. Anyway, your eyes will adjust to the dark, and you'll be able to see just fine."

Cassie held out a hand, and when Marcos took it, she gave him a friendly squeeze. "Just ten minutes," Marcos said.

"Just ten minutes," Cassie repeated.

They went downstairs and outside, where it had finally gotten totally dark. Mom stood on the patio talking to friends and neighbors who had come over for Dad's annual star party.

Marcos looked nervous.

"It's going to be great," Cassie whispered in his ear. She loved the night sky, just like her father did, and spent hours studying the planets and stars.

This year, Dad said she could be the one to tell everybody what they could see as they stood and looked at the sky with just their eyes. Then Dad would let their guests look through the big telescope to see things up close.

Marcos went over to stand by Mom. Cassie felt bad for him. She couldn't imagine being scared of the dark. When she looked up at the night sky, she felt so happy to see the stars. She loved to find the shapes the stars made, especially on a clear night like this one.

Everything was perfect. The pale new moon wasn't too bright. The stars that twinkled like diamond drops were easy to see. The November air was chilly, but not too cold. Cassie smiled happily when Dad asked her to come forward.

CHAPTER 3

The Stars Win

"Hi, everybody," Cassie said. "I'm going to show you my favorite thing first. It's the constellation called Cassiopeia, and it's my favorite because I'm named after it!" The guests laughed, and Cassie continued.

"The Cassiopeia constellation is made of five bright stars. They look kind of like a spread-out letter W. Look pretty high up and to the northeast. Can you see it?"

Cassie felt a tug on her hand. It was Marcos. "I don't see it. Can I go inside now?" he whispered.

Cassie bent so her head was even with her brother's. Now she could see things the way he did. "Look up and find the brightest thing you see," she said.

"I see something really bright over there," he said, pointing.

"That's the planet Jupiter," Cassie told him.

"We learned about the planets in school," Marcos said. "Jupiter is the biggest."

"That's right," Dad said. "Do you want to see Jupiter through the telescope?"

"First, I want to see Cassie in the sky," Marcos answered. "I haven't seen the W yet."

Cassie told Marcos to find bright Jupiter again and then helped him find the constellation from there. "I see it! I see a W!" Marcos suddenly shouted. "Can I look at that through the telescope, too?" he asked.

"Of course," Dad said, "but you've been out here for more than ten minutes. Do you want to go back inside now?"

"No way!" Marcos said. "I want to see what else is in the sky. This is really fun."

Dad smiled at Cassie and winked, and she smiled back. Marcos didn't mind the dark that night. The stars had won him over!

Summarize

Use important details to help you summarize *Star Party*.

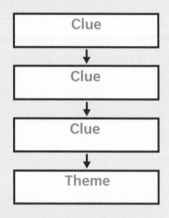

Clue

↓

Clue

↓

Clue

↓

Theme

Text Evidence

1. How do you know *Star Party* is fiction? GENRE

2. How does Cassie feel about viewing the stars? How does Marcos feel? THEME

3. *Star Party* uses a simile to describe the stars. What are the stars compared to on page 12? SIMILES

4. Write about the author's message about the night sky. WRITE ABOUT READING

Compare Texts

Read a poem about something else in the night sky.

Moon

Oh, I know that the moon is a rock,
Not a big chunk of cheese.
Men have walked on it,
But there's not a man in it.

Oh, I know that the moon doesn't shine
Like a flashlight.
Instead it reflects rays
From the sun far away.

Oh, I know that the moon isn't close,
Like next door.
But the full moon is beaming
As bright as a friend
In the shadowy night.

Make Connections

What about nature does Cassie find exciting?
ESSENTIAL QUESTION

What do Cassie and the boy in the poem have in common? **TEXT TO TEXT**

Focus on
Literary Elements

Repetition Repeating something, such as a sound, word, or phrase, is called *repetition*. Poets use repetition to make a poem sound more interesting. Repetition can also help to create rhythm.

What to Look for In *Moon*, the phrase "Oh, I know that the moon" is repeated. Sounds are repeated, too. The repetition of the first sound in a string of two or more words is called *alliteration*. *Reflects rays* is an example.

Your Turn

Write your own short poem about something you find exciting in nature. Use repetition in at least two ways: a sound, a word, a phrase, or a sentence. You may illustrate your poem if you like. Share it with the class.